Let's Roll

DIRT BIKES

by Wendy Hinote Lanier

FOCUS
READERS

www.northstareditions.com

Produced for North Star Editions by Red Line Editorial.

Photographs ©: dotshock/Shutterstock Images, cover, 1; Mark Sims/Icon Sportswire/AP Images, 4–5; i4lcocl2/Shutterstock Images, 7; Maciej Kopaniecki/Shutterstock Images, 9, 20; Library of Congress, 10–11; Edu Silva 2ev/Shutterstock Images, 12; Sonrak/Shutterstock Images, 15, 18, 29; sainthorant daniel/Shutterstock Images, 16–17; Maxim Petrichuk/Shutterstock Images, 22–23; lukovic photograpy/Shutterstock Images, 25; nattanan726/Shutterstock Images, 27

ISBN
978-1-63517-053-5 (hardcover)
978-1-63517-109-9 (paperback)
978-1-63517-210-2 (ebook pdf)
978-1-63517-160-0 (hosted ebook)

Library of Congress Control Number: 2016951019

Printed in the United States of America
Mankato, MN
July, 2018

About the Author

Wendy Hinote Lanier is a native Texan and former elementary teacher who writes and speaks to children and adults on a variety of topics. She is the author of more than 20 books for children and young people. Some of her favorite people are dogs.

TABLE OF CONTENTS

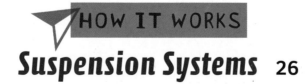

CHAPTER 1

THE DAYTONA 250 SUPERCROSS

It's race day at the Daytona 250 Supercross in Daytona Beach, Florida. The stands are full for one of the most important races of the year. The riders ease into the starting gate and rev their motors.

 Many dirt bike races feature large jumps at the finish line.

The gate drops, and the riders surge forward. Rider number 6 reaches the first turn ahead of the pack and claims the **holeshot**. He's in the lead. On the next curve, he **brake checks** the rider behind him in an effort to slow him down. The riders go over **whoop-de-dos** and around tight turns.

FUN FACT

Arenacross is an indoor version of motocross that uses smaller courses.

 Getting a fast start is an important part of dirt bike racing.

With only one lap to go, the leader nips the top of a jump. It slows him down just enough to allow number 34 to fly past him. The new leader skids around the next curve.

He sends up a **rooster tail** of dirt behind him. The crowd roars as he takes the checkered flag.

DIRT BIKE EVENTS

The American Motorcyclist Association (AMA) establishes racing rules for all types of motorcycle events. AMA racing series include supercross, motocross, endurocross, and dirt track. Each series includes a set number of races. Riders are awarded points for a race based on their finishing positions. The top point-getter in a series is named champion.

 A rooster tail can make visibility difficult for other riders.

CHAPTER 2

DIRT BIKE HISTORY

Motorcycles were first introduced in the late 1800s. At first, they were simply motorized bicycles. But by the early 1900s, companies were building motorcycles very similar to today's.

These motorcycles from the early 1900s are not much different from modern motorcycles.

Motocross jumps often send riders high into the air.

Companies began organizing races to test their latest models and interest buyers. The races became very popular. Soon, motorcycle companies were building special racing courses and bikes to race on them.

By the mid-1900s, cross-country racing was known as motocross.

ENDURO RACING

Enduro racing is a type of **endurance** test. The races take place over several hours or even days. Riders must follow a path over all types of ground surfaces. The objective is to maintain a certain speed throughout the race.

It featured breathtaking jumps and tight turns over rough outdoor courses. Originally called scrambles, these races tested a rider's ability to go over natural and man-made obstacles.

In the 1970s, a new type of racing called supercross brought

 Each race has a set number of laps that a driver must complete.

motocross into arenas and stadiums. These courses included high jumps, closely spaced bumps, and many turns.

CHAPTER 3

DIRT BIKE BASICS

Dirt bikes are off-road motorcycles. They are much lighter and easier to handle than road bikes. Most dirt bikes do not have windshields, lights, turn signals, or license plates.

A dirt bike race starts out with a large pack of riders trying to get the best position.

 Jumps often have large ruts that can make it difficult to control the bike.

This kind of bike is not legal to drive on the street. Engine sizes range from 50 cubic centimeters (cc) to more than 500cc. The engines are

usually two-stroke or four-stroke.

Two-stroke engines are lighter.

They work well on loose, sandy dirt.

Four-stroke engines are heavier.

They provide greater control in ruts

and on hard-packed dirt.

FUN FACT

Dirt bike goggles have layers of plastic sheets on them. During a race, a rider can tear off each layer when it gets too dirty to see through.

At some events, riders do tricks as they fly through the air.

Dirt bikes have a special **suspension** system for a smoother ride. Their large, knobby tires give the bike traction on all kinds of surfaces.

SAFETY GEAR

Dirt bike riders wear special protective suits, full-faced helmets, thick gloves, and heavy boots. Racing suits are made of leather. They are padded at the shoulders, elbows, knees, and hips. Each suit is custom-made. For some events, a steel plate on the left boot helps the rider slide through turns.

CHAPTER 4

TODAY'S DIRT BIKES

Dirt bike racing is a thrilling professional sport. But it's also a sport that just about anyone can do. Riding the trails off-road can be a family adventure or a favorite activity with friends.

 Riders sometimes put their feet down for balance.

Today's dirt bikes enable skilled riders to do outrageous moves. Advanced suspension systems, disc brakes, and better four-stroke engines have made this possible.

The most popular dirt bike makers are Honda, Yamaha, Kawasaki, and Suzuki. They

FUN FACT

In the early 2000s, pit bikes became the latest dirt bike craze. These small bikes have 50cc four-stroke engines.

 Most dirt bike riders do the sport as a hobby, not as a profession.

produce bikes with various engine sizes and a variety of frames. Some are designed for professional racing. Others are strictly recreational bikes that make off-roading fun for everyone.

SUSPENSION SYSTEMS

Dirt bikes have two suspension systems. The front suspension is made of a fork attached to the front wheel. Each side of the fork has springs that move up and down as the bike goes over bumps. Inside the spring is a fluid-filled strut that helps cushion the impact.

The rear suspension is a spring and strut combination attached to the bike's frame and rear wheel. These systems help the rider maintain control and increase speed.

Suspension systems help riders handle their bikes on bumpy tracks.

FOCUS ON
DIRT BIKES

Write your answers on a separate piece of paper.

1. Write a sentence that summarizes the main idea of Chapter 4.

2. Do you think children should be allowed to ride dirt bikes? Why or why not?

3. When did supercross first appear?
   A. the late 1800s
   B. the early 1900s
   C. the 1970s

4. Why don't riders use regular motorcycles in motocross races?
   A. because regular motorcycles are too slow
   B. because regular motorcycles are too heavy
   C. because regular motorcycles are too expensive

5. What does **traction** mean in this book?

    A. bump

    B. grip

    C. dirt

Dirt bikes have a special suspension system for a smoother ride. Their large, knobby tires give the bike **traction** on all kinds of surfaces.

6. What does **recreational** mean in this book?

    A. done for a long time

    B. done for money

    C. done for fun

Some are designed for professional racing. Others are strictly **recreational** bikes that make off-roading fun for everyone.

Answer key on page 32.

GLOSSARY

brake checks
When a rider slows down quickly, causing the rider behind him or her to do the same.

endurance
The ability to continue riding in spite of strain, pain, or difficulty.

holeshot
When a rider is the first one to reach the first corner of a race.

rooster tail
A spray of dirt behind a motorcycle.

suspension
A system of shock absorbers and springs that help maintain a smooth ride.

whoop-de-dos
Large bumps on a dirt bike trail, also called whoops.

TO LEARN MORE

BOOKS

Hamilton, John. *Dirt Bikes*. Minneapolis: Abdo Publishing, 2014.

Monnig, Alex. *Behind the Wheel of a Dirt Bike*. Mankato, MN: The Child's World, 2016.

Polydoros, Lori. *Dirt Bikes*. Mankato, MN: Capstone Press, 2010.

NOTE TO EDUCATORS

Visit **www.focusreaders.com** to find lesson plans, activities, links, and other resources related to this title.

INDEX

A

American Motorcyclist
   Association, 8
arenacross, 6

B

brake check, 6

D

Daytona 250
   Supercross, 5
Daytona Beach, Florida, 5

E

endurocross, 8
engines, 18–19, 24–25

G

goggles, 19

H

holeshot, 6
Honda, 24

J

jumps, 7, 14–15

K

Kawasaki, 24

M

motocross, 6, 8, 13, 15

S

safety, 21
supercross, 5, 8, 14
suspension, 21, 24, 26
Suzuki, 24

T

tires, 21

W

whoop-de-dos, 6

Y

Yamaha, 24

Answer Key: 1. Answers will vary; **2.** Answers will vary; **3.** C; **4.** B; **5.** B; **6.** C